Deno
    I'll Ask her tomorrow
And if she says yes, She
says yes. el doubt that
she will improve but
I will see what kind
of a girl she is.
    It she does improve
And I like her after
that. I don't know
what I'll do.
    You said that
you Did things with her.
what kind of things

Charles":

It was to nice what
I did!
Debbie likes you!
You should Go with her
and find out how she
is, then you can break
up with her if you don't
like her, and still go
with her if you do!

Penéo":

2gether 4ever

NOTES OF A JUNIOR HIGH SCHOOL HEARTTHROB

Dene Larson

CHRONICLE BOOKS

SAN FRANCISCO

Library of Congress Cataloging-in-
Publication Data available.

ISBN: 0-8118-4303-3

Manufactured in China

Book design by Benjamin Shaykin
Typeset in HTF Gotham
Handlettering (cover & pages 3-6, 8-9, 39,
70-71, 92, 94-96) by Melaina Bergin

Distributed in Canada by Raincoast Books
9050 Shaughnessy Street
Vancouver, British Columbia V6P 6E5

10 9 8 7 6 5 4 3 2

Chronicle Books LLC
85 Second Street
San Francisco, California 94105

www.chroniclebooks.com

2gether 4ever

Introduction

Junior High School. Hormones are knocking at the door. You've got your eye on Susie but Susie likes Charles, who likes Mary. Mary likes you, but wait, who's that? Cindy. Yes, Cindy. . . .

The only way to take measure of Cindy's heart is to tear out a sheet of binder paper, write "will you go with me?" make three boxes (labeled "yes" "no" and "maybe so"), fold it into a triangunote (see page 92), pass it to Charles to pass to Cindy, and wait.

Passing notes was an art form. Just folding them required an intense concentration unlike any other. From the giddy first crush to the heart-rending breakup, each roller coaster love affair was brokered and broken through these passionate notes.

Getting the guts to pass a note to someone that you had a crush on took incredible courage. Watching them read it, seeing their expression . . . wow! It was excruciating and wonderful at the same time, being so young and so in love, and wanting so desperately for the relationship to work out. You just knew that you'd fall in love, get married, and live happily ever after, all at age twelve. For up to a week it's sheer bliss. And then the heartache of the breakup. Getting a breakup note was the worst thing that could possibly happen, ever.

The notes in this book were passed among me, my friend Charles, and the many girls I loved during my junior high school years. They're a funny and sometimes poignant snapshot of the tortured soul of the junior high school romantic. Most of us are probably never going to wear our hearts on our sleeves as willingly today as we did back then. I've never been able to throw them away.

TLA,

Dene

I Like you,

Do you Like me?

Liz,

Do you think if I asked Sandy, that she will go with me?
I like her, she is nice. Nice and sweet, so I think she likes me, too. (hope so)

If you don't tell anyone else, you keep it a secret, call her or walk her home, and don't act like it's an every day thing. Tell her how you really feel, Yes!

Dean,

　　Your first compliment from Jane was "Oh, she's a tiny little girl (isn't she)" she thought you were a girl.

　　　　　　　　　　Toni Mill

Poo-Bear;

You know something?; I was just thinking about you in Bed so I got up and wrote you, I didn't think I would ever do something like that for you and I also didn't know I liked you that much. I wish I could see you more! I want to know something, Do you really like me As much as I like you? This might sound funny but I have a confession to make; I might sound a little big for my briches, but I do not mean anything I say most of the time. I cuss all the time to make people at school like me more! Dean? Do you promise you will not tell or say anything to noone untill we find out that there, if or is nothing different or the same between us? I promise? I understand what you mean by just being friend's but going together would probly be better for us! Do you still like Beth? Hope not! I put a picture in it's (anvelope) Hope you like it. Well my sister just walked in, so I gotta go! Gotta turn of the lights! Maybe I will dream about you tonight!!!!!!!!!!........

A H
O L (Hope) ?
(Hope so)

(SAVE ALL MY Kisses for YOU) Hope

LOVE YA,
ME

P.S. I would sign my name but someone might find it!

Dear Charlesa

You are in MRS. Randall's class
reading ~~thing~~ this note, I trust!

In P.E. We Probably won't dress
out! ~~████~~
Who do you like for real, I
like debbie and Teresa, I'm not ofcaid
to say so! You can like debbie
cause I'm not going with anybody!
Can you go to the dance, we
could probably pick up a coupla chicks!
ha ha ha, just a joke!

Sincerly
Deneo!

14

Dear Deno,

You better trust me to
Go to Mrs Randalls Room. I
Don't know what other boaring place
I should could go The reason why
I said boaring because we DO the
same boaring thing every week. Like
on Monday we Do spelling All period.
That's a boar. I could go on but I
Don't want to write you a Long net
because you never wrote me a
Long one.

F.
Charles

P.S. Bye

P.S.
Good luck on
the "Chicks"?

5/5/5.

Dane,

Hi how are you I'm fine
Were you really cheating? If
you were going today die I'd
get out of here because I
would have to much sorrow.
Would you come to my
funeral If I died. Well I'll
                              Love ya,

                                 Cindy

P.S. I LOVE
YOU
there I said
it are you
HAPPY!

To: You

Im sorry but
I cant get
you any-
thing for
Easter for
these
reason[?]

From Mes

P.S.
Call
Tonight!

Dene,

What's the matter? Did the dog die? If it did tell me how. Doe you still like Rhonda? I don't know who I like now. Well write back.

P.S
are you
going to the   your friend
Spring Concert   Debbie Kiness
tonight? I hope
so but don't laugh
at me if you go because
I hate that dress!

Dene

I'm gonna write this
letter all week &
I'm gonna beat yours!
Is Charles really gonna
go with Debbie Rivers?
And is she the one that
cussed you out. Why
did you breakup with
her. Well I guess I didn't
write this all week so

Bye!

P.S. Why did you breakup
with her just to go
with ugly me &
Dawn & Scott are
breaking up because
Scott said its like having
a girl & never seeing
her. But Dawn still loves
him. I hope we never
breakup. Dene, I care for
you more than anyone else
in this world well I have to go!

Bye

Love
Cindy

my P.S. is
bigger than
my letter
& Sandy doesn't
like Charles

Do you want a
piece of candy
I don't know,
I guess so, if i can
Here it is

Deno,
I don't know what
Debbie thinks about
me. I hope nothing
because I sure hope
wouldon't like saying
wait and we will see
what Developes Later.
F
Charles

I like Charls song
MARCY said Cindy was
Fat. Did you know Cindy
Debbie, was mad at
Do you like you?
Charles? You keep
Writing notes to
him.
I like you as a
friend.
I am going with
Someone named Cindy.

Dene

P.S. :- Do you like
Charles?

Debbie
from
Deno.

yes, Cindy may be
fat, but she is real
nice.
Yes, I know
Charles is mad at me,
but he started it!
It started yesterday
he locked my books in
the locker and it took
5 minutes to open
it! oh.
Stupid Charles!

Changing the
subject, huh?
No, I'm just
telling you the fads.

Are you going
to ask her?
Probally. Now you
understand the only
reason I'm going to
is because you
want me to.
uhhuh, you really
like her and you
know it! not her looks →

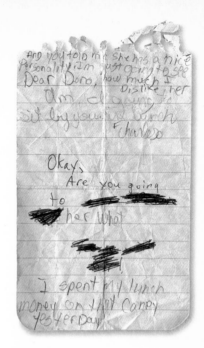

And you told me she has a nice
personality. I'm just going to see
Dear Dora, how much I
                        Dislike her
I'm cleaning
out by your lunch
                    Charles?

Okay,
Are you going
to ~~ask~~ her what ~~~~

I spent my lunch
money on that candy
yesterday.

Dear
What do you think
Sandy will say your
honest opinon.
Probably yes. But she
flirts with Ronnie Stewart, and
he flirts with her. Is Ronn
Stewart The Black
Dude That Rides our
Bus
That gets off at my
stop. I don't know
where you get off
only where you get on
well, get on I mean
I'll kill him just
Kiding ha!

Since you like that girl on the
bus, why don't you talk to
her. You might get her to like
you

as a
friend

Besides she
Just to young
and imature

Dear Dono,

Hi, how's the weather over there? Guess what, I get to go to the movie Friday night. That movie is going to be good.

Did Marcy break up with you yet? You two look like a good couple.

Sandy and David looks like a good couple. They get along good. Don't you agree?

Is Marcy going to the movie? How about David and Sandy? What about Bobby?

Do you still like Bobby? He was criticizing you yesterday along with Cindy. Not just a little.

I got a new lunchbox. I just wanted something to put my lunch in. I was tired of bags. I particularly don't like what the lunch box looks like. Wow, Wee, Eviel I never. ha ha ha.

Got to go.   Bye

F.

Charles

P.S.
Can I see the note Marcy gave to you

Dene,

    Yes, I like Charles as a good friend,
I also like you, Forrest, David as good
friends. Sam is ..... so, so. (If you know what
I mean)
No, I'm not going with anyone,
but I want to go with someone
who I like <u>alot</u>. He's in 9th grade.
You guys are real nice and you're
very good friends of mine.

For all you guys							
Love Line	never	yes	no	yes	✓	not really	No
							yes!
	Don't like	Friend	like a little	like pretty much	like very good friends	love	Love a lot	9th Rick

Why did you write that note?
It ok. but why?
Oh well see ya,

LORI

Why?
Why what?

Don't you like me Why

You've got too many girlfriends, I don't have 1		
Only 2 like me alot	You can 3 have	I don't want 3. I want One
Well take one! who		
Who are you going either	Janet Johnson	ask them if they'll go with you!
to give me other than Janet	Teresa Peterson	one at a time
Teresa, Kathy, Tony Miller	or Kathy Odom	I don't like them
Forget it. Who else	I don't know. who do I like?	who do you like?
I got Debbie, so you	I don't like you	Why
cain't have her! I wasn't	why what?	why Don't you like me
Plan on having her she is	like who?	me who?
...ject. Who else that's	Why don't you like Charles Fletcher?	
all that like you and me!	Charles, I like you	
speak for yourself, honey	One look at you, she'll run	
I'm not youre honey	away and I'll never see	
I have my eye on some one	her again	who?
but the problem is that	I can't see out of that eye	
I can't see out of that		
eye. Who? I'll		

get her
to like you

I Don't
        like you
    that's good

What does
she look
    like?
Pretty, ugly
cute short
tall fat skinny

I Don't
    like you
that's good

I won't tease
you about her!
won't laugh
I Don't know her

can't you get the message I
Don't have my eye on some one,
It was a Joke. liar, No No
It was a Joke, liar liar liar
    you like Debbie? NO. Do you like
anyone? Yes. WhO? Me, My Mom
My father but not Dero' So you do
like debbie or anyone else; ??
    In what form. G in Grene, Grene, or Girl
    ☐   ☐   ☐   ☐   ☐
  Teresa   Kathy   Debbie   Janet   Tony
            Just   who do   you like
    better? Who's Kathy, Janet

Kathy odom
   Tonja   Map of Gladestone's Room
        Kathy   If this is a map of this Ghestone
              Pinnt Room. Where is Mr Glastone

    🚗 me   🔲 Debbie
    🔲   🔲 you
    🔲 Janet   🔲 mark
    🔲 Donna   🔲 Pat
    🔲 Dennis   🔲 James

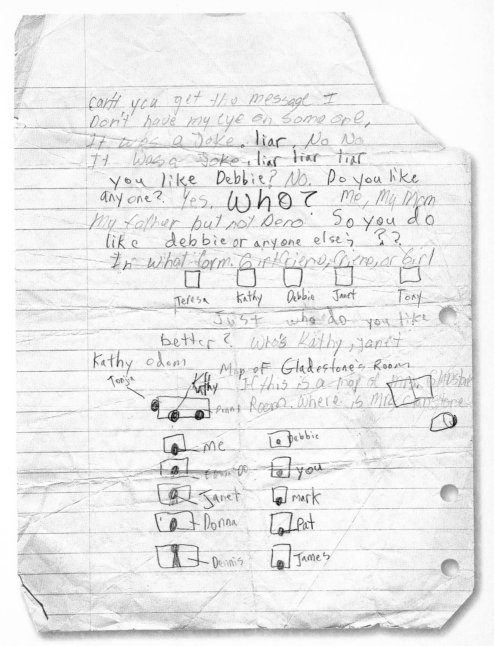

Will you

go with me?

Debbie,

Rhonda broke up, so I guess
I will go with you.
(if you want to)

Yes   NO

☒   ☐

I'll   I'll
Love   hate
you   you

Love,
Dave

P.S.- Go to the afternoon
movie tomorrow. (on base)
are you going to the movies?
If not, why?
How about Saturday night?
I have to go swimming
Saturday. And I'll be gone Friday

and Sat.
afternoon
so I won't
probably be
able to go to the
movies. Maybe, I don't know.
Dena Pete try to make it this time. KO?

TO: You
From: Me

Dene,

Hi. What's up. Nothing much here. I like you too. Ever since the ball game with Sandra P. Yes I will go with you. I guess Darrell Parrish is right. You don't have to act like a 8th grader, just act normal. Are you going to the games friday and Saturday? I am. They are both at 6:00. Sit on the writer side of the bleachers this time. Well gotta go.

Love,

Susan

W/B

Dear K.C.,

What are you going to answer?
Tell me now, so I will know.

Dene

what the hell does
G.S. Stand for

I don't know yet
so I will tell you
on the bus later
on, or something.
You must be
crazy wanting to
go with me. I don't
see why you like me
I won't see you but
on the bus or in school
because I am on restricktoin
and I wouldn't be able
to talk to you or see ya
for two or more weeks
OK. Its your Desion

O.K. seeya

31

Hey Dean
I will go with you sure but tell
Kelly that i said no okay she read the note.
Dean the bet we had was not for money
or any thing like that well I got
to go see Ya

Love
Ya
Denise

P.s. W/B/S
r   g   o
i   e   o
g   t   n
h
t

S/S/S
o   o
r   o
r   p
y   p
y

L/L/L
o   E   A
n   t   t
g   t   e
e   e   r
r   r

Denise
Ta - N -
Dean Ta

I hope
it stay
that way!

If you
Like me

286-5101
Don't call to
night Okay

Dear Tag (alias Dean)

~~Why I~~   Why did you
say that I was going
I didn't
→ with you to all your friends
You wouldn't have the privilege
of going with me!! All you
are is a wonton a toad on
the earth! You are
also a faggot!

Toni

Dear Gene,

My answer to your question is still the same. I can't explain it because it's to hard. It's not none of those things you said. Even if you keep asking me my answer will stay the same. I'm sorry. Pat told me that all the girls you asked said yes. Well I'm the first girl to say no. Good-bye for now.

Beth

Charles о,
     don't forget
to ask Debbie to
go with you!
(to see what
she is like)
   anyway, Beauty
isn't what counts!
Personality counts a
lot!

     Dene "o"

To: charles
From: Dene

Dene,
     Some times Beauty
counts.

Dene,
     That wasn't nice for
leaving me behind with
Debbie. You better not
do it again. No matter
what the consequences are.
If I wanted to walk
with her I would of
slowed down and waited
for her. I didn't so I
didn't want to walk with
her. She isn't very
pretty and I'm not sure
about her personality. over

she has more against
her than for her.
     Why did you go with
her. Because somebody
wanted you to or she has
is or was good looking to
you or did she have a
so nice personality. Tell
me the truth.
     The thing I'm faced
with is my friend which
is you, wants me to go
with her. If I do decide
to go with her I wouldn't
do anything with her. Charles

I don't know what he
said. **What did
Bobby C. say
about me?!**

I don't know, what
did he say?
Is it a funny joke?
No, In that note
yesterday you said he
said something
about me.
What did he say?
I don't know!

Who are you going with
noone
Do you want to go with
me? O.K.
Do you want to sit by
me in lunch
Where?? At my
table?! I guess
What about Denny?
We can sit by him
and Cindy. At my table
**What did Bobby
say about me?!**
Bobby said yes.

Ann, if you say I asked you
at the Roller Rink you're sadly mistaken
because David Parrish asked you for a
JOKE! Not even I knew about it!

Let me tell you something
I didn't say that you
asked me 3 times. I don't
give a damn if you asked
me once ~~and because~~ I was
not lucky because you are
chicken as hell!!
x friend ann.

Make-out city

Dene,

Hi, You
can come over
and sit on
the car Port
if you want
to.

Love,

Susan

Dean,

How is everything! Its O.K. here. I'm writing this note because I was wondering how you and Cori are doing. Are you going skating this Friday, with Cori. I hope you can do the bang bang with Cori! You haven't broken up with her did you? I haven't wrote a letter in a long time! So I thought I would write to you. You know that I like to skate now that I go, so answer my question about going skating Friday, OK! I'm a bad writer! Write back to me later, O.K.

BYE!
o——oo

your friend
Darla

41

Dene,

Hi there, whats up? whats down?
nothing here both ways. I recieved
your note from Down. I will get
off at the second bus stop. I'm
sorry I havent written many
notes but you know how it is.
I'll tell you if I want you
to put your (arm) around me.
Tomorrow I will bring my
lunch, and I mean a lunch, Lunch.
I'm sorry I keep on cracking up
but I was born that way.
I'm in a very good mood today
So you better watch out. well
I should + must be going
Bye Bye

→ P.S. What

Dene

I DON't HAVE
TOO TEll YOU
Anything.

Hi there, How ya doing,
Sine here (sort of)
Im so upset. Because dene
I am a not stubbern
I Just Don't want you
to kiss me.

Rhonda

PS Please
Don't break
up

Cori,

If its true what that girl said (no) about breaking up if I hadn't tried anything (no), I would've kissed ya but you would've caught my impetigo. (ew) (You probably didn't want me to kiss you anyway, right (maybe)) Kirstin said you didn't like kissing (no) (uvo) (she knows) so I figured you didn't.

Whatcha been doing (nothing)? What did your dad say when you hung up the phone last night (nothing)? Did he tell you he wanted to kill me (no)? Or mangle up my bones (no)? You better not tell him (im scared of him,) or then he'll tease me (right).

My mom thinks you are nice (good). she said she only said those things about you around Tina (Gustafson) because she didn't want to lose a friend (oh). she thinks you are nice (good). so does my dad (good), and Gwendolyn does (good) too!

Tonight will be fun, when we are skateing. Are you going to couple skate (yes), I want to learn to skate backwards (same here).

Is SNOb... I mean Kathy going (no)? I hope not. Well... she should ... I'm hoping to see her fall flat on her a... I mean butt (oh)

Dene,

    Hi there, whats up?
Nothing here. Im in Miss. Phillips
class. Were having a Filmstrip, Its
really stupid, I mean really stupid.
You have to read out loud. I wish
their was something to talk about
on the bus. Maybe we can think
of something. Im sorry about what
happened on the bus yesterday about
you know what. Its almost my turn
to read. Im even scared to read
out loud. I gooft again. I read
to fast. I can hardly see the
board. I hope I can get to the
lunch room ~~earlies~~ sooner then
~~usual~~ usual. Well I have to go
now. solong.

               Love
               Rhonda

                    P.S Love ya

Dene,

       Hi there, How's ~~life~~?
Well, I read your note in first
period, and decided to write
you right back. Dene I'm
NOT BORED With you. If
I was I would of told
you And besides Dene I don't
care if you don't put your
arm around me because as you
Know I'm not that type. Because
when someone tries to put
their ARM around me I get
chicken fever. (I'm Chicken)
   ~~sorry~~ But thats how I am.
I hope you arent mad. Please Don't
Be. We can have alot of fun
like ~~jolly~~ sitting ~~by~~ By each
other on the ~~bus~~ bus which we
already ~~why~~ do. I don't mind
you holding ~~it~~ my hand at a
movie and putting your hand
around me at a movie but
please don't do it around people that
can see us like in the lunchro
hallways. over

Dene please understand.
Now, I ~feeling~ feel like
I'm boring you, Because I
won't let you do anything. So if
you want to Break up please do I
don't wan't you Bored. Well I've
got to go. Please tell me on what
you decide.

P.s. I don't want you to break up
because I love you.

W/B/S

Love

Rhonda

47

Dene, Hi there. What's up? Well there's nothing going on around. Mr. Adams 4th period, boring. Why? cause that's Mr. Adams so this, I should be out of this bunch so I...

around me. and I'm still thinking about but that's the other thing. You may know the way it is. I should go want it. Mr. Adams note. because I dump I don't sit up

Dene
I don't like being called stubborn. just because I won't kiss you. That is pretty dumb. and I don't like you being mad at me over →

and I'm not going to tell you my personal problem so don't try to force it out of me well better go.
Rhonda

P.S.S I wish you would money for the game see ya on the bus this afternoon. I have a game tonight is it doesn't rain Love ya not forgot you

48

Tell me the truth Do you
not want to go with me
because you have never
made Out or anything
Well if you havent Do not
feel bad because I have
never ever kissed a guy
but ~~once.~~ one time.

49

Dene,

　　　Hi there, whats up?
whats down? Nothing here.
I'm in Miss. Phillips room
1st period. I really don't have
much time to write because
we have to write notes (alot)
well I'm done with my
notes its 8:26 right now
so I better hurry.
I might (lips) well better
go

　　　　　PS. Luv YA

　　　BYE
　　　　BYE

Dene,   Stay
                         Sweet!
          Hi, what's up?
Nothing much here? I'll be
back in a second! I *was*
just __kidding__, when I said
that at the ball park?
I couldn't meet you any-
way? Don't believe any-
thing Rhonda said? She
doesn't know if I ever
have done anything wild
a guy or not? I won't be
home this afternoon or night
because we are going to
Dothan, right after school!
You might make me
jealous if you keep hang-
ing around __those girls__, at
the ball park, after I
leave! Well I have got
to run! Bye!

          Love always, W/B/S

W/B/S

Phone number:
   286-5529

                    Susan

We're
breaking up

Diane,

Let's stop acting like a couple
little kids ok. ok. It's over
with ok ok.

Bye
Love,
Cindy

Dene,

I was fine untill I read your note. It is stupid to not like someone when you go with someone. If you break-up something will happen you will never forget. Dene I think You should stop acting the way you are acting! Why do you think people get married? Because they hate eachother you've got to be nut's. Going together is like getting marride, if you want it to be! It does feel like you are using me. Because you said you liked me and then you turn around say you dont love me no more and you me feel like an asshole. Who is making you feel tied down?

Love you always (I hope!)
(ann)

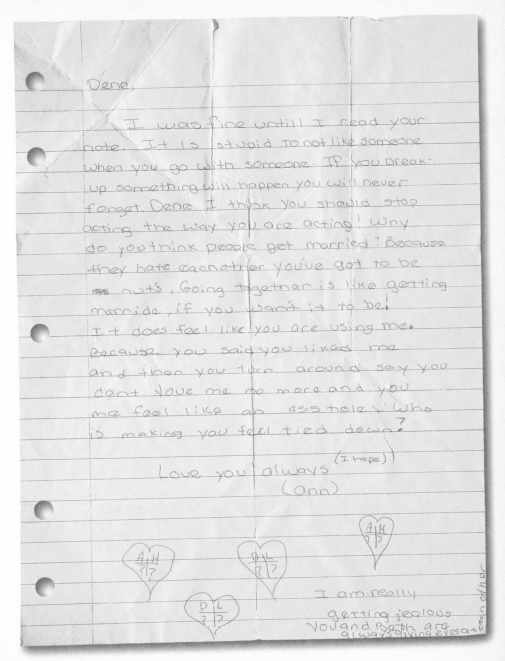

I am really getting jealous you and Beth are always giving eyes at each other

Dene,

Hey,
          I broke up because
you would talk behind my
back (bad things) you would
walk with other girls.
You Expect me of everything
like you thought I wanted you
to put your arm around me.
I do like you as a friend
but I just don't think it
would work out. well gotta go.
                    Atiose

                    Rhonda

P.S. your stuck up too.
     and your also a dummy, dummy.

Well is you don't care if I
break up, then just leave me
alone. because let me tell you
something I got someone next in
line too. (Good luck with Debie
Rivers. ──────> over

P.S.S I didn't break up
for Revenge.

Find one thing
else your the
~~user~~ user not
me. ~~Love~~ you
have done that to
every girl you
have gone with ,

April 12ᵗʰ 1976

Dene,

Hey there, just wait a second!
I wasn't that mean to you in Science
~~today~~ Yesterday. You dont have to talk about
my friends that way! I dont talk
about yours that way, except for
Bobby and you say he's weird too.
Would you quit saying "I love you"
Because you hardly even know me!
You just say that! Well dont say
it because I hate you and your
just a ~~fat~~ sissified bastard!
And I would like

don't go with Molly!
Becaus she's to good
for you. And besides
she wouldn't go
with you anyways, cause
your to big
of a sissie
In other words
your a
Woossy

P.S. W

B: if you know how!

OVER

Dont worry I wouldn't want
you to change your mind!
And dont tell me what to do!
Like "You can go with John again"
It sounds like I have to have
your consent to go with anyone.
And you can shove your big words
and spiteful jokes
UP YOUR
ASS!

P.S. Im not
a spiteful
person either!
(you are)

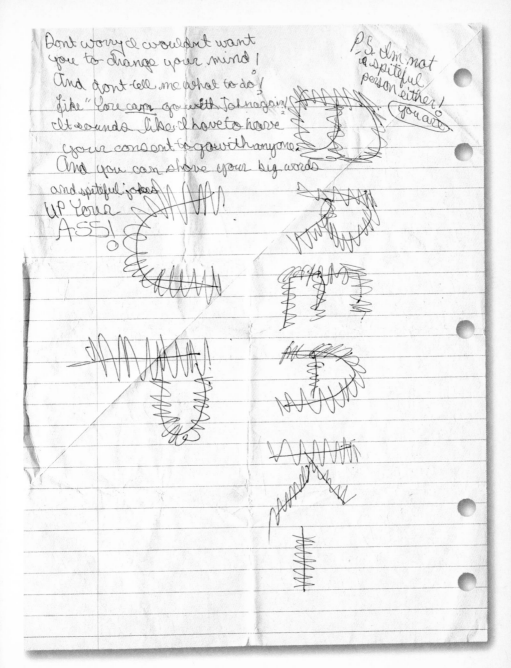

Dean,

Back in your mind you are screwed
up some where. You say one ~~when~~ thing
and contridict yourself by saying
something else. For instance
Quote " I didn't say I didn't like
you, I still do." unquote.
Quote "I believe Peggy because she
is one of my best friends, which
is more than I can say for you"
unquote.

What do you mean its a shame
I am so <u>rotton!</u>

If you feel I was using you
thats your own perogitive.

I am surprised to think you
had the act so "high + all mighty"
if I ask you a favor. It is not
using somebody when you ask
a favor. I ask my dog not to
do something and I'm not using
him. Like I said you better have
a talk with your self and find out
what your problem is.

~~Its~~ probably nothing but

It could help.

If you feel tied down because you sharpened a ~~girl~~ girls pencil or threw paper away for her your mixed up man.

Bye, Bye, Ann

61

Dene
Please Lets
not fight or
argue

Just shut
up. Don't ask
"who" or "what"
I'm Breaking up
see nois I'm mad

Dena

I have to break up with you
because you called me friday and I
told you not to call because I can't
have boys call me. So my dad got
very mad at me. Now I don't
talk at all in any of my classes any
more. I almost could not go to a
swimming party Saturday. I was
very upset friday. But I have to
break up. Dena this dosen't mean I don't
like like you I still do but I think its
better this way. Please don't get mad
at me ok? I'm not going with Eric
either ok?   (I still hope)

                              your friend
                              Debbie
                              Kines

63

I'm breaking up!
Dene
I'm glad! But I'm sorry for being mean but we are broken-up! so I just wanted to say I'm sorry.
Love Cindy
P.S. Happy Anniversary!
Ask Charles if he wants to go with me! no

Some anniversary
I'm sorry to, but we are breaking up! You always stretch my words!
bye,
Dene
P.S.: some aniversary!

Charles said no
I like Sarpy

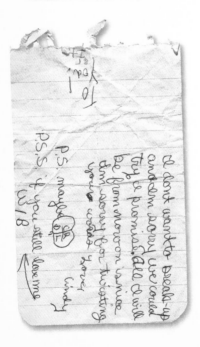

to you
P.S. maybe O.K.
P.S.S. if you still love me
W/B
I don't wantta break-up and am sorry we could try to promise I will be from now on I mine I'm sorry for twisting your words love Cindy

---

How did you guys get into this fight anyway.
She really took a picture from my math book, and ruined it. (it was Farrah) So I took her starsky and Hutch scrap book, and Drew vampire teeth on one in pencil! So she could have erased it, but now you can't even notice it! Ann told me about it but not very much but I'm not gonna take sides O.K? Cause me & you, Ann & I are finally friends & I wantta keep it that why! W/B.

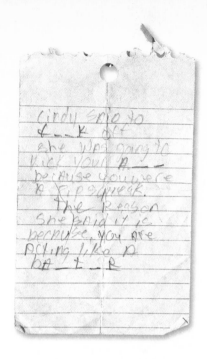

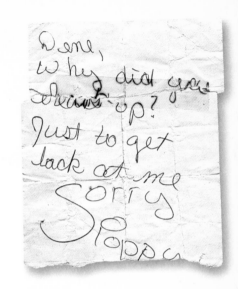

the dumb word. My ink is black yours
is blue look back Turkey!
I don't see anything Behind me but
ugly Chris. ha ha he Turkey!
It was funny wasn't It Turkey.
        Sure was Turkey
~~Gobble Gobble~~ - Gobble Gobble!
You must be going Crazy. Now you
sound like a turkey, Turkey!
        you mamma a turkey
All your family is a turkey
        My mamma and Daddy ain't but my
    hister is. I go Along with your
Sissy Sister but not your Animal
parents.
        I APOLOJIZE, you mamma
not a turkey, ... over
As Long as I'm not one
        you a nice kiddo
I'm a man, you Woman
        yah, a Faggy man
You a ~~Chip~~
C

She A BABOON !!

Dear Deno,

Hi. Hows the weather over there. The reason why Sandy broke up with me is because the only reason she was going with me is because Cindy was going with you. I had the same idea of breaking up. But I was going to wait untill thursday so it would be one week even.

Are you going to let me see the note Cindy wrote to you. I can see the note from my seat that you are writing to her. All I see is Fat Face. ha ha.

Got to Go. Bye

F charles o ♥

P.S Write back sometime

Yes   here it is!
Read mine, too!

Dene,

Hi, and how are you?
I'm doing okay! Dene we
aren't getting along to good!
The point is I want to
break-up! I thought it
would work out at first
but it isn't! Sorry
but you will meet
other girls in your time!
Bye-bye!

Your
freind,

Susan

P.S. We can still be
friends can't we?
P.S.S. My secretary didn't
write this either!

I Hate You,

Let's Be Friends

Dean,

I can understand that you and me didn't get along to well? But maybe we can try it again sometime. I can also understand that you would get imbarrased and I whould to if we did do something right in the middle of the hall! I really don't get to see that much and I need to know you more. I wish you were taller it would have beenso much easyer then. Do you still like Beth alot? because I lika you still.(Hopeso)

Ann Holley

Friends again!!!

Don't let

Beth read

it.

O.K.

Whats do you mean by
I am not worth talking
to. You will never forget
this moment when I hate
your guts. see what NOT
Going together can do to
you? Take Beth and
stick her up your
ass for all I
care.

You know something
you can really hurt
someone ~~tip~~ ~~to be~~ deep
down cant you!

I hate
you.   (I wish not)

YOU.   ANN.

(but I will
Always love
you.)

74

Dene,

I'll save this seat for you.
Why did you break up with Ann?
She really likes you. You are the
only one she talks about during
second period. Sorry this is messy
but I usually print. I read one
of those letters. She's really mad
now. I don't see why she should
be. I mean you still want to be
friends, don't you?
    I did see the movie "Norman is
that you?" It was good. It was
about some Homos.

See Ya Later
Peggy Owens

Dene,

I was insulted because always say Darlene! Shut up! Carol doesn't have to do anything "you say" I get fed up with it you did this after I offered you the money. You act like this about your stories you let Donna and Teresa read but not me you snap off me.

Laura

P.S. Your friend

Allison,

I'm sorry I kicked you, but I don't feel very good today.

I don't like to be mad at people, especially you.

I don't care what you do with this, throw it away if you want, but I'm sorry. I want your friendship. let's be friends, okay?

Dene.

P.S.:- write back if you want to be friends. I guess so! You know every once in a while Everyone has to blow of steam I guess today is your day! AS

Dear Deney,

I'm not mad at you. I like you, you're a good friend of mine. I'm sorry about Sunday. But thank you for ~~other~~ coming anyway. I like you, John Grant and John P. you're all good friends. that's all. Sorry I didn't write back before 4th or 5th. <u>Are you mad at me now?</u> F Hope not. Sorry this is so ~~soso~~ sloppy I wrote it on the bus. I also like a bunh of other box, but there just friends.

Love Teresa

P.S <u>S o r r y</u>

I made you mad

P.S.S. I still like you. Are we still friend?

To Dene

Sorry
If I
made
you
mad. Teresa

Teresa,
    I'm not mad at you any more
but I sure am going to rememember
that!!
    I'ts nice about the trophy!
I Bet John is heartbroken, I think
John is a "nerd"!
    Its too bad, I'm going with
Someone in our Science class, where were
you?
    When you wrote a P.S. you
went like This;
    P.S. I'm, your'e what?

       Ex-Love,

         Dine

Dear Deno,

Hello. Watcha doing on the other side of the table? How's the weather over there. The sun is shining of here.

How do you feel for beeing a batcheler for once. I know that you will grab a girl before the day is over with. You might even grab the same girl.

Who else do you have in mind? Is it Cathy. Do you still think Debbie is spitful. Debbie can't understand anything. I hope she hurries up and find her a boyfriend. I don't want her to bug me.

I don't have much more to say. But how did you like that play

F Charless

P.S Write Back

Dear Denö",
  Hello" there. How's the weather
over there. You never gave me an
answer about my girl in Ohio. What
should I do.
    Hey, did you know that my
cousin came down this weekend. His
name is Berry. He's my dad's brother's
son. He's a real cool guy. All he
did this week was playin tennis, went
swimming, and went fishing. He did that
All week, every day he did the same thing.
    I always am good in 2nd period.
I don't have to be good to be good
because I'm the best, (I would put
an ha,ha but it's true).
    Who do you have in mind to
"grab" now. Don't grab her to
fast. You've got to have patience.
I know that every time it comes
to girls you're a beasty animal.
But this time you aren't going
to act that way. Aren't you. Is you
do you are going to be "disgusting" read
in Paul Lynn's voice). (Ah,ha). Bye
                    F charles "ö"

Dane,

Lori Mc. made up a lot of fibs to me about her and Brian. Lori said this down by the swing to Sherry that she had enough of me! I've had enough of Lori. I can't stand her! Lori is making up a bunch of fibs about Holly. Because Holly is getting more famous than Lori! I CAN'T STAND LORI MC. Shes a fag and a half! Scott hasn't asked me to go with him yet! Who ever said that the girl couldn't ask the boy to go with her? I'd like to know.

always,
Kathy

P.S. Write back soon!

P.S.S. Love can be forever but yet its a very short thing.
P.S.S.S.

83

Dene,

Hi, What's up.
I'm over at the Fryers.
Babysitting. Rkanda
really does like you
but she is afraid you
don't like her because
she acts wild. She was
jelous when I was
going with you. Let's
still be good friends
Okay? Okay!

Your
freind,
Susan

W/B

Dere
from
Susan

Eve told me
of word

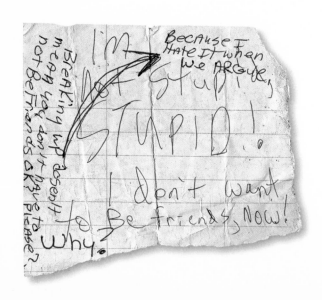

Dene,

Hi there. How ya doing?
Fine here. I'm in Geography with
Mr. Edwards 6th period, and I decided
to write because I don't have the
chance at home, if you know
what I mean (Mom + Dad)
There isan't much to say but
I'll try to think of something.
O.K I've thought of something.
Are you going to the softball
game tomorrow? I am. Also
I hope you get a good grade
on your Geography test. I had
a test in my Geography class
yesterday. This note is probaly
boring, so I'll close for now.

R | B
D | L I A

Love
Roanna

P.S. What do you have 1, 2, 3, 4,
5, 6 periods?

Dear Deno,

Hello.. Do you still like me. I Hope you Do. Who are you going to ask next to go to the Dance with you. I can't got for 3 reasons, no girl, no suit, And no permission from my mother. At Least I Don't have a money problem.

The real problem at the Dance will be Animals. You Know How much room they need to Dance. Wouldn't It be funny if somebody was doing the Dance called "Kong fu fighting" and they gave you a karate chop to the neck. that would be nice. You Know why. Because the things you said about me in the Note in Mrs. Sad Rock's Class were Disgusting. The bell is about to ring So I'll Say So Long

Charles

P.S. Bye

Oh. Charles, Just wear a nice shirt and nice pants, and There will be girls AT the dance, they will surely dance wi us! Ask your mother, my mother will let me go! Do you want my mom to call yours, and we can go to the dance together! It will be Fun!

All animals aren't mean, some are pretty nice! They don't ~~take~~ take up that much room!

I want to go, and I want you to go, too!

we'll meet girls there!

I Didn't mean to say that, you teased me, too!

OF course I Still like you!

Dene

Dear Deneo
    Hi
      F.
    Charles o,
      Hi
       L.
       Deneo
        From

Farrah + Cheryl...

ugly

... which looks Better?

F. - ⫫⫫⫫⫫⫫⫫⫫⫫⫫⫫⫫⫫⫫⫫⫫⫫⫫⫫

C. - √

Dean, write me a note cause I want to write you back.

How to make
a triangunote

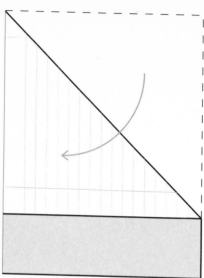

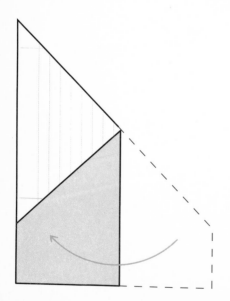

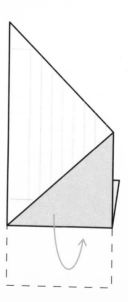

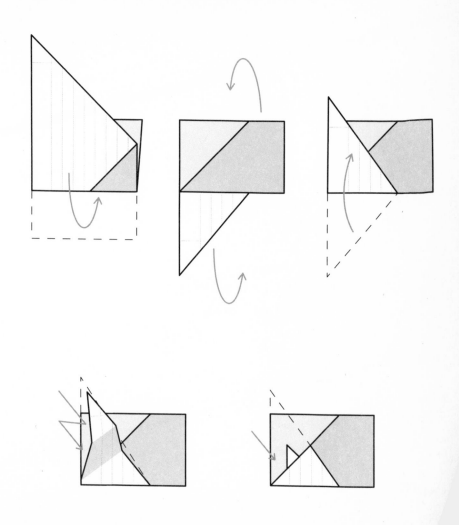

Note-speak

Use this glossary of note-speak to pass your own notes.

2G2B4G	Too Good to Be Forgotten
BFA	Best Friends Always
BFF	Best Friends Forever
BYOB/BYOG	Bring Your Own Boyfriend/Girlfriend
CTN—ML	Can't Talk Now—More Later
DGC	Don't Go Changing
FF	Friends Forever
HOLLAND	Hope Our Love Lasts and Never Dies
JK	Just Kidding
KIT	Keep in Touch
LLL	Longer Letter Later
LYLAS	Luv Ya Like a Sis
MM@L	Meet Me at Locker
OOC	Out of Control
QT	(cutie)
RO	Rock On/Rock Out

Sorry So Late	**SSL**
Sorry So Sloppy/Sorry So Short	**SSS**
Spin the Bottle	**STB**
Stay the Same	**STS**
Sealed with a Kiss	**SWAK**
Sealed with a Lick 'Cuz a Kiss Won't Stick	**SWALCAKWS**
Sealed with Glue 'Cuz a Kiss Won't Do	**SWGCAKWD**
True Friends 4 Ever	**TF4E/2F=4E**
Too Good For You	**TGFU**
True Love Always	**TLA**
True Love Forever	**TLF**
Ta Ta For Now	**TTFN**
Talk to You Later	**TTYL**
Very Funny	**VF**
Write Back If You Want	**WBIYW**
Write Back Soon	**WBS**
You're a Superstar	**YASS**

 Dene Larson grew up all over the United States and Canada as an Air Force brat. He now lives in San Francisco.

Do you like this book:

A Little ☐

A lot ☐

Just as a friend ☐